A Month in the School of Mary

Reflections of an Exorcist

Fr. Gabriele Amorth, S.S.P.

A Month in the School of Mary

Reflections of an Exorcist

Fr. Gabriele Amorth, S.S.P.

Translated by Bret Thoman, OFS

Icona Press
Peachtree City, Georgia

ICONA PRESS

True knowledge of Mary leads to unity;
every mother is a source of union between members
of the same family.
Unity is a gift from God that must be obtained with
much prayer;
and for this reason it is necessary to continuously
beseech the intercession of Mary.

Therefore, I invite you to say the beautiful prayer of
Brother Roger Schutz of Taizé:
"O God, you willed to make the Virgin Mary
the image of the Church. She received Christ and
gave him to the world.
Send your Holy Spirit upon us
So that, soon, we shall be visibly united in one body
and because we radiate Christ to men who cannot
believe."

Father Gabriele Amorth

Contents

How to Use this Book

This concise book was created for busy people who desire to carve time out of their schedules for personal meditation. It is designed so that they can stop for a few minutes, take stock of their lives, and then get back to work.

The book consists of short reflections and texts, one for each day. Each week is introduced by invitations—the synthesis of the text itself—that can be used as a refrain throughout the day. The headings of each reflection are the work of the author of the book, though you, the reader, can rework them and transform them as you see fit, so as to make them your own. The goal is that they become part of your daily life, like bookmarks.

At the end of the week, when perhaps you have a little more free time, give yourself a time for more prolonged prayer. Here, there are prayers and written reflections. Reflect on them. Then recall each of the invitations, considering them as extracts from the wisdom of the author, and apply them to what is going on in your life. Bring them into your thoughts, struggles, doubts, joys, and feelings of the week that has just passed.

Next, use the space provided to jot down what comes to mind. The result will be a kind of diary. From an anthology of Father Amorth's thoughts, the words will gradually transform into a diary of your own soul, which you can revisit periodically in the future.

Finally, for those who wish to delve deeper into Father Gabriele Amorth's thoughts on Marian meditations, there are four broader proposals at the end of this booklet, one per week.

WEEK I: MARY, HUMBLE AND GLORIOUS MOTHER

In this immense Kingdom of which Christ is King, Mary has been elevated to the position of Queen, alongside Jesus, who crowned her Queen of Heaven and Earth. This is the glorious, final, and perpetual position of Mary.

We who invoke her do well. For, she loves each of us, as if we were the only person who existed.

The Seven Invitations of Week I

Monday: The Power of Mary.
Tuesday: Two Hidden Protagonists.
Wednesday: Exalt, with Mary, the Power of God.
Thursday: Pray to the Holy Mother of God.
Friday: Exult, Be Happy, and Rejoice.
Saturday: Fully Consecrated to God.
Sunday: There is No One like You.

Monday: The Power of Mary

In the divine plan of salvation, the Creator's thought and love for the Virgin Mary, or rather for the one in whom the Incarnation of the Son of God would take place, had to have been present.

The Immaculate Virgin, the fruit of whose womb crushed the head of the tempting devil, was united with the Son in the struggle to definitively defeat the adversary.

The Mother is totally united to the divine Son in the work of salvation, as Vatican II reiterates: "[The Virgin] she devoted herself totally as a handmaid of the Lord to the person and work of her Son, under Him and with Him" (*Lumen gentium* 56). Still today, the Son and Mother are united in the struggle against evil in the world, in particular by supporting the ministry of exorcists.

Tuesday: Two Hidden Protagonists

Mary pondered on the words of Gabriel in the Annunciation. (See Luke 1.) To communicate to her that the birth of her child would be miraculous, the archangel conveyed to her the example of the miraculous birth of a sterile woman. He could have cited other well-known examples, such as that of Sarah, Abraham's wife. Instead, he cited the contemporary condition of a relative of Mary's, Elizabeth. This caused Mary to consider that there was a relationship between her Son and Elizabeth's son. Moreover, Gabriel specified that Elisabeth was in her sixth month. Why? Perhaps this was to communicate that Elizabeth, in her old age, needed help in the final three months.

Elevated by God to such unique greatness, Mary strongly felt the need to serve. She deeply felt her humility. Gabriel had already revealed God's plan, when he announced the birth of John to Zechariah six months earlier. Mary understands the relationship between these two announcements and runs to where God's plan began.

The visitation between Mary and Elizabeth had two "hidden" protagonists: the children they both carry in their wombs. The greeting that Mary addressed to her elderly cousin is not specified in the Bible. I believe it was "*shalom*," which means, "peace be upon you." Her greeting causes the Holy Spirit descend on Elizabeth, who exclaims in a loud voice: "Most blessed are you among women, and blessed is the fruit of your womb. And how does this happen to me, that the mother of my Lord should come to me? For at the moment the sound of your greeting reached my ears, the infant in my womb leaped for joy. Blessed are you who believed that what was spoken to you by the Lord would be fulfilled" (Luke 1:42-45).

This is such a rich response, which demonstrates a total revelation of the Holy Spirit to Elizabeth. The first fruit of Mary's simple greeting is the gladness with which John leaps for joy in his first meeting with Jesus. These are the two protagonists of that visit. But it was Elizabeth who was the first to recognize that the child in Mary's womb was the Lord, that is, her God.

Wednesday: Exalt, with Mary, the Power of God

Mary responds to Elizabeth with the wonderful hymn, known as the Magnificat, or the Canticle of Mary (see Luke 1:46-55). This is the only time Mary speaks at length in the Bible, which she does to exalt the power and mercy of God. The heavenly Father's exaltation of Mary leads to a long exclamation: "My soul proclaims the greatness of the Lord; my spirit rejoices in God my savior. For he has looked upon his handmaid's lowliness" (46-48). In this, there is also a tone of thanksgiving from her: she feels saved and lifted from her lowliness to the loftiest heights, above all humanity.

She then says, "All ages will call me blessed." (48). Why? Though she feels humble, "The Mighty One has done great things for me, and holy is his name" (49), great is his mercy, great is his might. She explains the power of God as the rebirth of all humanity, which exalts the lowly and disperses the arrogant. Indeed, he scatters the proud, throws down the rulers from their thrones, and sends away the rich empty. On the other hand, he lifts "up the lowly" and "the hungry he has filled with good things." It almost seems that Mary is anticipating the spirit of the

Sermon on the Mount, when Jesus delivers the Beatitudes.

Finally, Mary exalts God for his faithfulness to the promise he made to Abraham and to his descendants forever, extended throughout the earth: "In your descendants all the nations of the earth will find blessing" (Genesis 22:18).

Thursday: Pray to the Holy Mother of God

To be efficacious and succeed in his ministry of exorcism, as a witness to the Christian fortitude and hope that supports against all evil, the exorcist must be faithful to the daily Holy Mass; to the Liturgy of the Hours; and to intercessory prayers to the Holy Mother of God, the archangel St. Michael, and one's patron saint. Additionally, he must be constant in meditating on the Word of God—above all, the daily readings. From the New Testament, he should meditate in a special way on the Prologue of the Gospel of John (1:1-18) and the Christological hymns in the Letters to the Ephesians (1:3-14), the Colossians (1:15-20), and the Philippians (2:6-11). This is because Christ is more evidently present in this revealed Word. Jesus is the beginning, the center, and the end of the created universe—the One in whom all creatures are created: those celestial (the angels) and those earthly (living and inanimate beings).

Friday: Exult, Be Happy, and Rejoice

Mary was troubled by the angel's greeting. (See Luke 1:26-38). In fact, Gabriel did not address her with the common greeting, "*Shalom*," which means, "peace be with you." Instead, he said (in the Greek translation), "*Chàire*," which means, "exult," "be happy," and "rejoice." It was a well-known word, used only once by three prophets (Zechariah, Zephaniah, Joel), and always in a messianic sense. Thus, Mary wondered what relationship there could be between her and the Messiah.

Moreover, the angel did not call her by her name but said, "Hail, favored one! The Lord is with you." All this "greatly troubled" Mary, and she pondered the meaning of such a greeting.

Gabriel's subsequent explanation touched on her soon-to-be motherhood, the name of her Son that means, "God saves," his endless Kingdom, and other elements that indicated him as the awaited Messiah. On the one hand, Mary believed in everything that was said with simplicity. But on the other hand, she felt herself sinking into her humility. Yet, she gave her unconditional consent by declaring herself the handmaid of the Lord.

Then, the Holy Spirit intervened, and the Word of God became flesh within her. This is why we celebrate the Annunciation—that is, the Incarnation of the Word—on March 25, precisely nine months before Christmas, which falls on December 25.

Saturday: Fully Consecrated to God

God carefully prepared the two people to whom he entrusted his Son. At the moment of her own conception, Mary anticipated the fruits of Christ's redemption, and she was born without original sin. For this, we refer to her as truly the Immaculate Conception.

Tradition has it that Mary consecrated herself entirely to God when she was a girl. In this way, she is the "ever virgin," par excellence. It should be noted that in the Jewish world, there was no tradition of women making a similar choice. Before the example and words of Jesus, the Jews honored only motherhood. For a woman, sterility was considered a shame, even a curse. Furthermore, there was always the hope of being related to the Messiah: for Mary, the choice of virginity would have blocked such a prospect. Moreover, Mary was Joseph's wife, so Jesus was born into a family.

Sunday: There is No One like You

Elizabeth, at the Visitation, was the first person to call Mary the "Mother of God." She was also the first person to affirm that Mary is the most blessed of all women.

We also note that Elizabeth exalted Mary for her faith when she said, "Blessed are you who believed." This was in contrast to her husband, Zechariah, who, due to his unbelief, was struck mute until the birth of John.

These are the primacies (firsts) that make Elizabeth a great prophetess of the New Testament. I have no hesitation in referring to her as a "prophetess." She is certainly a prophet who spoke under inspiration by God, truly moved by the Holy Spirit.

PRAYER AND MEDITATIONS,
WEEK I

DELIVER US FROM EVIL

Lord Jesus,
If any evil has ever been done to me, my soul, my
body, my work, or my family, by your power, your
mercy, and your will, grant that from this moment, I
may return to full grace, complete health, perfect
union, and to the will of the Holy Trinity.

I ask this of you, O Jesus, through Your merits,
Your precious Blood shed on the cross, the pains of
the Virgin Mother
and the intercession of the patriarch St. Joseph.
To the glory of the Holy Trinity.
Amen.

HUMILITY

The first week is dedicated to contemplating Mary's humility; that is, to her way of being humble—a simple handmaid. It is precisely in the sweet simplicity of Mary that we encounter the loving and saving power of God. Mary is great because she is chosen; she is great because she believes; she is great because she makes herself available to what the Lord asks of her, without conditions.

Now we revisit the seven-day period and write down any reflections that have accompanied us this past week. We can also write down any inspirations we may have that lead us to abandon our own plans and, like Mary, follow the new and creative path as indicated by God the Father to his children.

MY THOUGHTS AND REFLECTIONS

_____
_____
_____
_____
_____
_____
_____
_____
_____
_____
_____
_____
_____
_____
_____
_____
_____
_____
_____
_____
_____
_____
_____
_____

WEEK II: MARY, THE MOTHER WHO FOLLOWS HER SON

The Lord spared her neither the pain nor the torment of not understanding. It is always painful for a mother not to understand her child.

Yet, Mary always trusted God with her eyes closed, without any pretense of explanation.

The Seven Invitations of Week II

Monday: The Strongest, the Most Beautiful.
Tuesday: A Poor Family among the Poor.
Wednesday: Mary Meditates in Her Heart.
Thursday: A Tormented Love.
Friday: Why Are We Searching for the Son of Mary?
Saturday: The Attentive Intervention of Mary.
Sunday: Mary, the First Cooperator of Jesus.

Monday: The Strongest, the Most Beautiful

Both the exorcist and the simple layperson can rest assured they are safe the more they are aware of being loved by God the Father, the Son, and the Holy Spirit and protected by the Holy Virgin Mary and the angels and saints. In short, they are on the side of the Strongest and the Most Beautiful.

God grants them every grace they need to face and overcome the devil. Everyone can respond to his menaces by responding, "I am enveloped in the mantle of our Lady. What can you do to me? I have the archangel St. Michael at my side. Try to struggle against him. I have my guardian angel who watches over me, and I cannot be touched. You can do nothing to me."

Tuesday: A Poor Family among the Poor

The first who came to pay homage to Jesus were not the rich but the shepherds; that is, they were the poorest and most destitute. (See Luke 2:15-20.) Pastors in that era were considered "second-class" citizens. They were believed to be unreliable and prone to thievery. They were not allowed to be judges, and their testimony was not considered valid in trials. And yet, God sent the angel to them to announce the great event: "For today in the city of David a savior has been born for you who is Messiah and Lord. And this will be a sign for you: you will find an infant wrapped in swaddling clothes and lying in a manger" (Luke 2:11-12). The shepherds immediately set out to go and honor the child.

The shepherds understood everything right away. The city of David was Bethlehem, [as it was close to Jerusalem and part of the Kingdom of Judah]. When they saw the child placed in a manger, they understood that although he was the awaited Messiah, alongside a particular relationship with God, he was also very poor, so much so that he was born in a cave equipped with a manger.

Mary and Joseph were delighted with the visit from the poor, who were not a cause of worry. While

the shepherds recounted what they had been made
known by the angel, Mary and Joseph rejoiced at the
gestures of God, who had favored the poorest for the
great announcement. The poor understand each
other, and whoever is poor is immediately ready to
help those poorer than him. When the shepherds
departed, it is probable that, without saying anything,
they left some milk and cheese, or milk-based
products, in a corner of the cave. This would have
been providence for the Holy Family, who at that
moment had nothing. Moreover, the shepherds
would have spread the joyous news among the
people.

Wednesday: Mary Meditates in Her Heart

The narrative of the shepherds at the cave ends with a particular observation, "Mary kept all these things, reflecting on them in her heart" (Luke 2:19). While others tend towards action, Mary tends towards contemplation.

Perhaps the evangelist Luke also wanted to reveal the source of this part of his Gospel. In fact, he says in the prologue that he wrote "after investigating everything accurately anew"; that is, as he says shortly before, going back to "eyewitnesses." (See Luke 1:1-4.) All these facts of the infancy and childhood of Jesus, at the time Luke was writing, in Jerusalem were known only to Mary. They could have been narrated only by her.

Thursday: A Tormented Love

The messianic importance of the narrative of the finding of Jesus in the Temple is given by Mary's question and Jesus' response, "Son, why have you done this to us? Your father and I have been looking for you with great anxiety" (Luke 2:48). Note that Luke, referring to the term "with great anxiety," uses the same word that he uses to present the pains of Hell. They were truly "hellish" hours for the parents.

Perhaps Mary intended to ask, "Was there a particular reason? What have you decided to do now that you are about to become an adult?" (In that era, children were considered adults at thirteen.) "What should we do?" Who knows how many questions Our Lady asked herself during that very painful period of darkness.

Friday: Why Are we Searching for the Son of Mary?

Jesus' response to Mary and Joseph, after his discovery in the Temple, contains the first spoken words of Jesus handed down by the Gospels. They are words that are so rich in meaning that they could not be understood immediately: "Why were you looking for me?" (Luke 2:49).

His response was not a reproach but a way of making himself understood. It is a reference to the sacrifice of the cross, when the angels will say to the women who go to the tomb, "Why do you seek the living one among the dead?" (24:5).

Jesus then goes on to say, "Did you not know that I must be in my Father's house?" (2:48). That is, when Jesus was forty days old, he was offered entirely to the Father in his house, in the Presentation. In this, there are three points to consider:

1. "that I must be…" Obedience to God is an imperative duty and superior to obedience to parents.

2. "in my Father's house…" What concerns God is contrasted with what concerns the parents.

3. "My Father…" In response to "your father," mentioned by Mary. This comparison does not

demean Joseph, but recalls reality and the absolute precedence that belongs to God.

Saturday: The Attentive Intervention of Mary

Perhaps Mary, who arrived first at the wedding at Cana, was a relative of the bride or groom, and she had come early to help with preparations. (See John 2:1-12.) She demonstrates some authority in giving instructions to the servants. Jesus was also invited, and he came with his first disciples. He probably arrived just as the wedding began. It is worth considering that not all the guests could participate in all seven days, which was the length of wedding feasts in that era, and there was a certain amount of coming and going of people.

Certainly not immediately, but after a few days Our Lady realized that the wine had run out. This would have been a major disruption to the wedding and could have seriously humiliated the spouses. Hence Mary's thoughtful intervention with her Son: "They have no wine" (John 2:3). Then there was Jesus' response, which has puzzled biblical scholars: "Woman, how does your concern affect me? My hour has not yet come" (John 2:4).

Sunday: Mary, the First Cooperator of Jesus

Jesus responds to Mary at the wedding of Cana with the term "Woman." He sees his Mother in the context of the Kingdom of God that began with him. Mary is no longer an earthly mother; rather, she has a fundamental role in the New Testament. She is the woman already announced in Genesis, as the Mother of the new humanity. She is the victor of Satan, united with her Son, to crush the head of the serpent. (See Genesis 3:15). She is the new woman, crowned queen of Heaven and Earth, in the final kingdom where Jesus is the supreme King. (See Revelation 12:1-2).

Let it be clear that Jesus is the only mediator between God and man. But so that his work reaches all people, Jesus needs us. His first cooperator is Mary, then the apostles, then the rest of us, including parents who educate their children in the faith, parish priests, missionaries, and all who pray and offer their sufferings in union with the crucified Christ.

PRAYER AND MEDITATIONS, WEEK II

A PRAYER AGAINST CURSES

Lord our God, O Ruler of the ages, omnipotent and
all-possessing,
You who made everything
and who transform everything with Your will alone;
You who in Babylon transformed the flame of the
furnace into dew seven times more ardent and You
who protected and saved Your three holy children;
You who are the doctor and physician of our souls;
You who are the salvation of those who turn to You:
we ask You and invoke You to nullify, drive away
and put to flight every diabolical power,
every satanic presence and machination, every evil
influence,
and every curse or evil eye of wicked people
performed on Your servants.

We pray that instead of envy and evil, abundance of
goods, strength, success, and charity may follow.

You, Lord who love all people,
stretch out Your mighty hands
and Your most high and powerful arms,

and come and aid and visit this image of Yours,
sending upon it the angel of peace, the strong
protector of the soul and body,
that will keep away
and banish any evil force, poison, or spell
of corrupting and envious people; so that under
You, Your protected suppliant may sing with
gratitude to You:
"The Lord is my helper
and I shall not fear what man can do to me. I will
not fear evil because You are with me, You are my
God,
my strength, my mighty Lord, the Lord of peace,
father of future centuries.

Yes, Lord our God,
have compassion on Your image
and save Your servant from any harm or threat that
come from evil spells
and protect him by placing him above all evil;
through the intercession
of the most blessed, glorious Lady, the Mother of
God and ever Virgin Mary,
of the resplendent archangels and all Your saints.
Amen.

FORTITUDE

The invitations of the second week are aimed at dispelling discouragement at the difficulties related to following the Son. In Him, Mary knows she finds the path to holiness. In Him, she finds the joy of living, serving, and interceding fearlessly as at the wedding at Cana.

Now we revisit the seven-day period and write down any reflections that have accompanied us this past week. We can also highlight any difficulties that arise in following Jesus, such as moments of discouragement or loneliness. Let us not forget to look to Mary and the way in which she confronted difficulties on her own journey.

MY THOUGHTS AND REFLECTIONS

WEEK III: MARY, MOTHER WHO PROTECTS HER CHILDREN

O August Queen of Heaven and Sovereign of angels,
you who have received from God the mission to
crush the head of Satan,
we humbly ask you to send us celestial legions,
so that in your presence they may chase off demons,
fight against them, repress their audacity, and repel
them back into the abyss.
Amen.

The Seven Invitations of Week III

Monday: The Most Beloved Prayer to Mary.
Tuesday: Mary, Mediatrix of all Graces.
Wednesday: Mary is the Reason of my Hope.
Thursday: Under the Protection of Mary.
Friday: The Prayers of Mothers.
Saturday: The Vast Power of Prayer.
Sunday: Marian Pedagogy.

Monday: The Most Beloved Prayer to Mary

The Rosary is the most beloved prayer to Our Lady, and it is a very powerful weapon against the devil. Thus, I highly recommend it to all who suffer from spiritual ills. This prayer has, in fact, a strong power of protection and liberation from evil.

One day, Sister Lucia, one of the visionaries of Fatima, revealed that God has given such great power to the Rosary and there is no evil—personal, family or social—that cannot be defeated by its recitation, when prayed with faith.

Tuesday: Mary, Mediatrix of all Graces

"In the end my Immaculate Heart will triumph." This prophecy of Mary was given in Fatima. It reassures us that—in the face of rampant sin and before man who has abandoned God, considering him a heavy obstacle to his unbridled freedom—the tribulations of the Church will come to an end. And the end will be good: God will have the final word over history.

The struggle against the devil, that is, exorcism—an earthly anticipation of the eschatological struggle between the Mother of God and the ancient dragon (see Revelation 12)—cannot do without her. For this reason, Mary is always invoked during the rite of exorcism. During the prayer, the priest repeatedly invokes her intercession and her powerful action. Without her, little is accomplished in the struggle against Satan. The one who does the freeing from the devil's influence is always God—this is worth repeating—but he has a completely unique ear for the mediation of Mary, the Mother of the Son.

What role does the Virgin have in liberating the obsessed? Mary, as the Hail Mary says, is "full of grace." She is the mediatrix of graces before God in favor of all people, particularly those who suffer most

And do not those who suffer from spiritual ailments suffer most?

Her mission, therefore, is consistent with her role as universal mediatrix of all graces. The enmity between Mary and Satan—solemnly proclaimed by God in the first book of the Bible, Genesis (see 3:15), and manifested in the eschatological struggle with the dragon—makes her the devil's principal enemy. But she will crush his head in the end of time.

Wednesday: Mary is the Reason of my Hope

For twenty-six years, from 1942 to 1968, I regularly went to San Giovanni Rotondo to meet with St. Pio of Pietrelcina. The friars usually have signs over the doors to their cells with scriptural verses. Over Padre Pio's door, there was this: "Human greatness always has sadness as its companion." Its meaning seems clear to me: we must have humility, a lot of humility, just as Jesus had in living what Paul defined in no uncertain terms as "emptying" (see Philippians 2:7), that is, his becoming man—he who was God—and his death on the cross, having been rejected by men.

After this sign disappeared from Padre Pio's door, another was placed. This one said, "Mary is the reason for my hope." If Mary, who is the Mother of Jesus, is our hope, then anyone—those who suffer, those who are alone, those who feel sad, or even, I dare say, a Muslim—can look to the Lord's Christmas and to his Easter resurrection with a heart full of hope.

Thursday: Under the Protection of Mary

"*Sub tuum praesidium confugimus.*" (Under your protection, we take refuge.) This is the most ancient invocation to the holy Mother of God. Entrusting ourselves to Holy Mary is the sure road and in some ways the simplest for those who want to keep themselves from the devil.

We turn to Mary because we feel the need to be protected from all dangers. The history of the Church, her saints, and Christian peoples reveal a constant devotion to Mary, who touched the highest peaks in moments of trial and most painful circumstances. She has always been considered the refuge in difficult times.

To the devil, Mary is the invincible one. I myself asked the devil several times during exorcisms why he was so afraid of her. His response is invariably the same: "Because she always conquers me, she has never been tainted by the slightest shade of sin."

Paul VI wrote, "All that struggles against sin struggles against the devil." This is why the devil is so afraid of Our Lady. She cannot be touched by sin.

We only need to read the Bible to understand. From the beginning, Mary is associated with the fight and victory over the devil: "I will put enmity between you and the woman, and between your offspring and hers; They will strike at your head, while you strike at

43

their heel" (Genesis 3:15). She is presented again in the struggle against Satan in the book of Revelation:

> A great sign appeared in the sky, a woman clothed with the sun, with the moon under her feet, and on her head a crown of twelve stars. She was with child and wailed aloud in pain as she labored to give birth. Then another sign appeared in the sky; it was a huge red dragon." (12:1-3)

Genesis and Revelation—the first and last books of the Bible. The struggle that was initiated at the beginning of time will last until the end of time. This is highlighted in *Gaudium et spes*: "For a monumental struggle against the powers of darkness pervades the whole history of man. The battle was joined from the very origins of the world and will continue until the last day" (37).

Friday: The Prayers of Mothers

If the intervention is not human, the devil is blocked. In the same way, he is blocked when confronted with people united to God, of strong faith, of a life of prayer, of a particular predilection of the Almighty, of devotion to Our Lady, or of a special grace, perhaps received through the intercession of some saint. In these cases, a person is protected.

At the same time, there is no doubt that one's mother's prayers also apply to the child she carries in her womb. Thus, a life of faith; of closeness to God; or of entrusting oneself to Our Lady, to the saints, to one's guardian angel, or to the blessings of tahe priest also serve as protection from the devil for one's son, who prays through his mother. It was once believed, in fact, that a child born to a baptized woman was also baptized. The mother's consecration to God was also valid for her child, flesh of her flesh.

Saturday: The Vast Power of Prayer

The Lord has given us many graces to overcome the devil, such as prayer. Prayer has vast power. It is the triumph of good. There is also a life of the sacraments, entrusting ourselves to the protection of Our Lady, and unconditional trust in Divine Mercy.

I am often asked if Our Lady was ever tempted. Of course, I reply, she was tempted all her life. However, she was always victorious over Satan's efforts. Often in exorcisms, demons openly report this sense of defeat before Our Lady. They are angry with her, and they fear her because she has conquered them and is always victorious over them.

Sunday: Marian Pedagogy

Every [Marian] apparition, even while illuminating all humanity throughout history, is linked to an historical moment. The messages that are given have particular relevance to what is most needed by society at that time or in the immediate future.

Following the thread of apparitions, their messages and consequences on history, a true Marian pedagogy emerges. It is as if Our Lady has taken us by the hand and guided us along the paths of life, pointing out the dangers and snares, helping us to carry our crosses.

In the constant struggle against the devil, Mary never misses an opportunity to have us understand that she is on our side and that it is enough to rely on her intercession to always emerge victorious. More concretely, in fact, Our Lady shows us the ways we have, in our humility, to ward off evil, to avert it for ourselves and for all humanity.

PRAYER AND MEDITATIONS, WEEK III

A PRAYER TO MARY MOST HOLY

May the Virgin Mary
preserve us and our families from every attack by
the Evil One—physical, mental and spiritual.

May she intercede with her Son Jesus, whose Blood
has redeemed the world and under whose Word of
life every knee bends submissively in Heaven, on
Earth, and under the Earth.

May the Immaculate Virgin ward off the dangers of
darkness, whose false strength breaks helplessly
against her blessed mantle under which every child
shelters.

Amen

SPIRITUAL PROTECTION

The third week leads us to reflect on the protection of prayer, particularly Mary and the holy Rosary. The many trials and evils we face—seemingly for the first time and alone—Mary overcame and conquered by totally entrusting herself to the fatherly love of God.

Now we revisit the seven-day period and write down any reflections that have accompanied us this past week. We turn to Mary with confidence. She—a woman who knew suffering, Mother of Jesus and our Mother—never abandons us in our moments of trial and temptation.

MY THOUGHTS AND REFLECTIONS

WEEK IV: MARY, MOTHER OF ALL

Every privilege was given to Mary for a reason
beyond her personal sphere. Even the Assumption
does not fall outside this criterion.
In fact, the Assumption was not granted to Mary
solely to honor her person but in light of a salvific
event.

In the Assumption, Mary received a new mission
from Jesus, which will last until the end of the
world: Motherhood over all, ordered toward
salvation.

The Seven Invitations of Week IV

Monday: The New Woman.
Tuesday: With the Aid of Mary.
Wednesday: Mary Gives Humanity the Fruit of
Life.
Thursday: God Gives Each of Us a Task.
Friday: Mary, *All Holy.*
Saturday: What Good Can Come from Nazareth?
Sunday: A Model to Imitate.

Monday: The New Woman

When the Church celebrates the Feast of the Nativity of Mary on September 8, the liturgy recalls the dawn, the rising of the sun; that is, the birth of the Virgin is a prelude to the birth of Jesus. The Second Vatican Council expresses this with a beautiful phrase regarding the birth of the Virgin. Chapter 8 of the Dogmatic Constitution on the Church, *Lumen Gentium*, is dedicated entirely to the Virgin Mary. It states, "With her the exalted Daughter of Sion, and after a long expectation of the promise, the times are fulfilled and the new Economy established" (55).

All was created in light of Christ: the role of every creature, of each of us, already present in divine thought from all eternity, depends on this Christocentric approach. If the firstborn creature is the incarnate Word, then the one in whom the Incarnation would take place could not fail to be associated with him, before any other creature, in divine thought. Hence, there is a unique relationship between Mary and the Holy Trinity, as is clearly manifested in the Annunciation.

Tuesday: With the Aid of Mary

In Fatima, the Virgin stated: "In the end my Immaculate Heart will triumph." What does this mean if not that we need to always trust in the Lord and in Mary's maternal aid?

There is especially the danger of discouragement. This can affect everyone but, in the case of spiritual maladies, it is even more pernicious because the results can often be slow to manifest. This means that, with the aid of Mary, we must commit ourselves to allowing ourselves to be converted by God—to know how to do his will, which is always ordered toward forgiveness and love. We must learn how to make every event an opportunity for sanctification and the fulfilment of God's plan in our lives.

Mary leads us to Jesus because she was the first to allow herself be intimately touched by the Holy Spirit, begetting Jesus in time.

Wednesday: Mary Gives Humanity the Fruit of Life

There is a centrality to Christ and his coming as the Savior. All human history is oriented toward the birth of Jesus, who is called the "fullness of time." The previous centuries were known as the "time of waiting," while the subsequent centuries are known as "the end times."

With the birth of Mary, human history fulfills the great turning point: the period of waiting ends, and the period of fulfillment begins. She is the new Woman, the new Eve. From her comes the Redeemer, and the new people of God begins.

Early Church Fathers, such as St. Justin and St. Irenaeus, took delight in drawing a comparison between Eve and Mary. Eve was the mother of the living, while Mary is the Mother of the redeemed. Through Eve, humanity receives the fruit of death; through Mary, humanity receives Christ, the fruit of life.

Thursday: God Gives Each of Us a Task

God has considered each of us from all eternity. He has assigned us a task and brought us into this world at the right time and in the right place, providing us with the tools necessary to carry out this role.

This is what he did with Mary. Wishing to entrust her with an extraordinary task, he prepared her properly.

We can summarize this preparation in three words: Immaculate, Virgin, Spouse.

Friday: Mary, All Holy

The first gift—the great gift that God gave Mary at the moment of her conception—was in making her immaculate, that is, applying the merits of Christ's redemption to her in advance. She was to become the Mother of the one who came to destroy the works of Satan, that is, sin and all its consequences. Thus, Mary, conceived immaculately, reveals her equality with us because she, too, needed to be redeemed through the sacrifice of the cross. On the other hand, her immaculateness predisposes her to the highest mission, which was then entrusted to her.

One of the oldest Marian titles, which is particularly dear to Orthodox Christians, is *All Holy*. It expresses well the two aspects that it intends to represent, invoking Mary Immaculate.

The first is that of pure privilege, that is, the exemption from original sin given her divine motherhood. Here we have only to contemplate the marvels worked by the Lord. But there is more.

There is a second aspect in which it is stated that Mary never committed the slightest actual fault despite being an intelligent and free creature. Contrary to how it might seem, in this, we touch on Mary's imitability, which can be beneficial in

Christian formation: in Mary we see the beauty of human nature pervaded by grace. The Immaculate Conception is an ideal that draws us; it does not blind us. The figure of Mary does not push us away; rather, it invites us to imitate her with baptismal grace, with actual graces, in the struggle against sin.

Saturday: What Good can Come from Nazareth?

Among the most likely sites for the honor of Mary's native city, Jerusalem and Nazareth are the two most probable places. There are ancient traditions suggesting both, with evidence based on archaeology and devotion. I am inclined to suggest Nazareth, since it is there where we meet this humble girl, enveloped in hiddenness. Away from the main roads and lines of communication, Nazareth is not mentioned in the Old Testament, that is, the Talmud, or by Flavius Josephus [the Roman-Jewish historian]. "What good can come from Nazareth?" (John 1:46), as Nathanael would say to Philip.

Nor do we know with certainty about Mary's lineage and which of the twelve tribes of Israel she belonged to. Certainly, it must have been a humble tribe; otherwise, St. Luke would have told us, since he goes to great lengths to describe the lineage of Elizabeth and the elderly Anna—the other two women he speaks of in the infancy narrative.

It is clear that God cherishes humility and hiddenness. He doesn't know what to do with human greatness, with what is considered great in the eyes of men.

Sunday: A Model to Imitate

One of the greatest faults against humanity in modern times is that of wanting to remove the sense of sin and the terrible presence of Satan. In this way, redemption—the victory of Christ over sin and the devil—is not recognized. In this way, man is left fallen in his misery and is not aided to rise again, to improve, and to regain his original beauty as a creature made in the image of God.

But the Immaculate Conception tells us: "I am this way because of the grace of Christ and because of my response. You, too, must strive, by responding to grace, to overcome evil and to purify yourself more and more."

The Immaculate Conception is not an abstract ideal to be contemplated; she is a model to imitate.

PRAYER AND MEDITATIONS, WEEK IV

PRAYER AGAINST EVERY EVIL

Spirit of the Lord, Spirit of God, Father, Son, and
Holy Spirit, Holy Trinity,
Immaculate Virgin,
angels, archangels, and saints of Heaven, descend
upon me.
Mold me, Lord, shape me, fill me with Yourself, and
use me.
Cast off all forces of evil; annihilate them and
destroy them so that I can be happy and do good.
Drive away from me all evil spells, witchcraft,
black magic, black masses, hexes, bindings, curses,
evil eye, diabolical infestation,
diabolical possession, and diabolical obsession,
everything that is bad, all
sin, envy, jealousy, perfidy,
every physical, mental, spiritual, and diabolical
illness.
Burn all these evils in Hell, so that they never touch
me or any other creature in the world.
I order and command,
through the strength of Almighty God, in the Name
of Jesus Christ the Savior, through the intercession
of the Immaculate Virgin, to all unclean spirits,

to every presence that harasses me, to leave me
immediately,
to leave me definitively and go to eternal Hell,
chained by St. Michael the Archangel, by St. Gabriel,
by St. Raphael,
by our guardian angels, and crushed under the heel
of the Most Holy Virgin.
Amen.

IMITATING IN LOVE

In the fourth week, the spiritual image of Mary becomes a model to imitate, an original beauty to discover, and an invitation not only to become better but to be what we were born to be: beloved children ready to love. Mary is like this by grace and by choice.

Now we revisit the seven-day period and write down any reflections that have accompanied us this past week. Mary's maternal gaze makes the fear of being misunderstood and despised flee from our lives. Those who concern themselves with pleasing only God, like Mary, fully trust in his help, enjoying his goodness every day.

MY THOUGHTS AND REFLECTIONS

_____

_____

_____

_____

_____

_____

_____

_____

_____

_____

_____

_____

_____

_____

_____

_____

_____

_____

_____

_____

_____

_____

_____

Further Marian
Reflections by Fr. Amorth

I. In Joy and in Pain

(An Excerpt from *My Rosary*)

The childhood of Jesus adhered to the customs prescribed for Jewish children during that time. Eight days after his birth, he was circumcised to confirm his belonging to God's chosen people. During this occasion, he was named Jesus, as revealed by the angel. Forty days later, he was presented in the temple as a ransom, and his Mother underwent the rite of purification.

The ransom of Jesus had a different meaning from the purpose for which the rite was instituted. In commemoration of the sparing of the firstborn in Egypt, it was believed that the firstborn of the Israelites belonged to God and needed to be redeemed. However, for Jesus, there was no need for redemption. His parents presented him to God in obedience, fully aware that he already belonged entirely to the Father. Moreover, his Mother, who had entirely offered herself to God, was united with her Son in this recognition. Furthermore, God united Joseph and all humanity with himself. God knew that he had sent his Son to reconcile humanity and bring all people back to him. He lovingly accepted Mary's complete offering.

Then came the brief ceremony of purification. Here, too, we find Joseph associated with Mary, although only Mary was required for this rite, which consisted of a simple prayer. Joseph was seen to take part, as long as he was alive, in what happened through Mary and through Jesus. On this occasion, the holy couple presented the prescribed offering of two doves, which was the offering of the poor. If they had been wealthy, they would have offered a lamb or a kid.

At this point, an unexpected figure is introduced. Surely, the elderly Simeon must have shared with Joseph and Mary that the Spirit had revealed to him that he would not die until he saw the Christ of the Lord, and that the same Spirit had led him to the temple. It was evident to Mary and Joseph that he was a prophet, and they willingly entrusted the infant Jesus into his arms.

Simeon gazed upon the infant with immense love and proclaimed, "Now, Master, you may let your servant go in peace, according to your word, for my eyes have seen your salvation." He then added a prophecy that warrants contemplation, stating that the child would be the "salvation of all peoples"—a light for all, not just for Israel but for everyone, as

God promised Abraham, saying, "All the families of the earth will find blessing in you" (Genesis 12:3).

Then changing his tone, he declared that Jesus would be a sign of contradiction for those who listened to him and for those who rejected him, and that he would bring about resurrection for some and downfall for others. Turning to the Mother, he added, "And you yourself a sword will pierce, so that the thoughts of many hearts may be revealed." Mary's life would be marked by the piercing of a sword. The sword symbolized not only an instrument of killing, but also of division. Mary's soul would feel the division of hearts—those who accepted the salvation of Christ and those who rejected it, even to the point of condemning Jesus.

These words were a painful revelation for Mary. She then realized that the life of Jesus would not be a constant triumph, as the promises of Gabriel on the day of the Annunciation suggested; these "glories" would come later. She also understood her role better. It was not limited to the birth and childhood of Jesus; instead, she would be his disciple for her entire life, through all the sufferings, until the end. Faced with this anticipation, Mary gave her complete "yes," just as she had given her "yes" to becoming the Mother of Jesus. Thus, Mary remains a model for us of continuously saying "yes" to God—in joy and in pain.

II. The Heart of Mary, Pierced by a Sword
(An Excerpt from *My Rosary*)

At this moment, John represents all of us as he "took her into his home"–that is, into his life as a disciple of Jesus who, before the mystery of the cross, embodies the entirety of the radicality that it entails. As disciples, we need certain things, such as the bread of life and participation in divine life, but we also need a Mother like Mary.

In the final act, Jesus gives us one last gift–he proclaims the motherhood of Mary for each of us. Her motherhood is very real and aimed at regenerating us in Heaven, directed toward our eternal salvation, and therefore necessary for us. To be reborn in Heaven, we need a Mother.

While reciting this mystery, I usually begin with a reflection before each of the ten Hail Marys, in which I recall the seven phrases proclaimed by Jesus on the cross with prophetic references.

First Hail Mary: "Father, forgive them, they know not what they do" (Luke 23:34). Not only does Jesus forgive, but he also seeks justification. May our forgiveness always be like this.

Second Hail Mary: "Today you will be with me in Paradise" (Luke 23:43). The words of the "good thief" are splendid. He acknowledges his faults, affirms the innocence of Jesus, believes in his royalty, and prays to him, "Remember me when you come into your kingdom" (Luke 23:42). It is not difficult to recognize Jesus when he works miracles. But to recognize him when one is a poor convict dying at his side would take heroic faith.

Third Hail Mary: "Behold, your mother [...] behold, your son." This was not [said] to deprive Mary of her motherhood, but rather to extend it to all of us. Jesus was communicating to his Mother the maternal mission she would have for the future. And he was telling us about the necessary aid to which we should resort. Just as Jesus chose the necessity of Mary to become incarnate as a man, he also chose Mary as the necessity for us to be regenerated in Heaven. This is why she follows and helps each of us along our earthly pilgrimage.

Fourth Hail Mary: "My God, my God, why have you forsaken me?" (Mark 15:34). This cry is not one of despair, but arises from feeling extremely beaten down. It is the outpouring of Jesus' humanity, which feels abandoned by God.

Fifth Hail Mary: "I thirst." The torture and significant loss of blood resulted in unbearable thirst. His mouth must have been dry, his tongue stuck to his palate.

Sixth Hail Mary: The prophecy has truly been fulfilled: "For my thirst, they gave me vinegar" (Psalm 69:22). He must have drunk it with avidity and then felt disgust.

Seventh Hail Mary: "They divided his garments by casting lots" (Matthew 27:35). This, too, was done by the soldiers. We note that the only possessions Jesus had left were the clothes he was wearing. With this, his poverty was complete.

Eighth Hail Mary: Now he could say with Job, "Naked I came forth from my mother's womb, and naked shall I go back" (Job 1:21). It should be noted that the Jews considered it repugnant for the crucified to be exposed naked. For this reason, Jewish women offered a cloth to wrap around the waist of the condemned.

Ninth Hail Mary: There was nothing left to say but "It is finished." That is, Jesus had done the will of the Father completely. He had fulfilled all the prophecies about him.

Tenth Hail Mary: "Father, into your hands I commend my spirit" (Luke 23:46). These are the final words of Jesus. He expressed them in a moment of great spiritual aridity, but of total and faithful abandonment. He came into this world sent by the Father, and now he leaves it to return to the Father. Throughout his life, Jesus always expressed his total dependence on the Father–in everything he did and everything he said.

Now, finally, he returns to the one who sent him. At this point, I usually add two mysteries. (I mention this only as an option for those who wish to do the same.)

VI Sorrowful Mystery: The most Sacred Heart of Jesus, pierced by a spear.

VII Sorrowful Mystery: The Immaculate Heart of Mary, pierced by a sword.

When Jesus died, darkness covered the earth. The apostles closed themselves up in houses in Jerusalem, fearful of being arrested as followers of someone who had just been executed. The pious women concerned themselves with going to the tomb to complete the embalming of Jesus.

However, Mary remained serene despite her suffering. She was the only one who was certain that Jesus would fulfill what he had said. No one else was thinking about the Resurrection, and no one else believed in it, despite the many announcements Jesus had made.

The faith of all humanity rests in Mary. She alone held the faith of the nascent Church, which would later be born glorious on the day of Pentecost.

This is why in many parts of the Catholic world, during the silence of Holy Saturday (which is defined as an "aliturgic" day; that is, the day when the Holy Sacrifice of the Mass is not celebrated), it is customary to celebrate the "Hour of Mary," a prayer centered on the faith of Mary.

The descent of the Holy Spirit is preceded by nine days of intense prayer, with Mary and others. The disciples pray in the temple or in the great hall of the last supper. Perhaps it was also a period of intimacy. Who knows how many questions they asked Mary about the birth and childhood of Jesus?

III. Mary Enveloped by the Infinite Love of the Father, of the Son, and of the Holy Spirit

(An Excerpt from *My Rosary*)

Now we arrive at the glorification of Mary, whom Dante defines as "more humble and sublime than any creature" (*Paradiso*, XXXIII, 2). Immediately after being called "Mother of God" for the first time by Elizabeth, Mary bursts into a song in which she reflects on herself: "The Lord has turned his gaze on my humility and made great things in me, and holy is his name." From this magnificent portrait that Mary presents at the beginning of her calling as Mother of God, we can contemplate the earthly culmination of Our Lady, when she was assumed body and soul into Heaven.

Pope Pius XII pronounced the dogma of the Assumption with the words: "The Immaculate Mother of God, the ever Virgin Mary, having completed the course of her earthly life, was assumed body and soul into heavenly glory" (Apostolic Constitution, *Munificentissimus Deus*, 44, November 1, 1950). The pope does not delve into the question of whether she died. This is an issue of personal value and does not affect matters of faith. After all, death is a universal human experience; for, even Jesus died. Therefore, there is no reason to assume that Mary, who lived a humble life, would have been exempt from death. Furthermore, the liturgical feast of the "Dormition of Mary," which has been celebrated for centuries in the Eastern Church alongside the Assumption, should not be silenced.

The Assumption of Mary is a profoundly significant event in the plan of salvation and it has immense salvific implications. Mary's role in the Incarnation of Jesus, as divinely ordained, was irreplaceable. However, Mary's mission does not conclude with her death. While her earthly mission pertaining to Christ required a humble and suffering body, her mission toward us, which persists until the end of time, necessitates a spiritual and glorious body, always intertwined with Christ. Scripture consistently attests to the unbreakable bond between Jesus and Mary during their earthly lives, making it logical to expect this bond to persist in their heavenly existence.

Christ's earthly existence was marked by the constraints of a mortal body, characterized by suffering and limitations. However, through his Resurrection, he experiences a new birth, obtaining a spiritual body free from human limitations and imbued with a glory and strength he did not possess before. This is the living and risen Jesus whom the apostles promptly proclaim to the masses and who is present in the Eucharist. Moreover, this transformation that Jesus demonstrates for himself and for us is a direct consequence of his Resurrection. It is not merely a simple transition from earth to Heaven, but a profound metamorphosis and glorification of the entire human being, encompassing both soul and body.

In relation to Mary, as she was chosen for her mission to the Son, just as the fruits of Jesus' Passion were anticipated to her, enabling her to be conceived without original sin, likewise, in anticipation of her current mission, the glorification of her body was granted. This is the essence of the Assumption: Mary participates in the complete glorification of her Son, being united with him in the work of universal mediation with the Father. As a result, she remains alive and present among us, adorned with the glory to which we are all called, and we look to her as the fulfillment of our hope.

Assumed into Heaven, Mary was immediately enveloped in the boundless love of the Father, the Son, and the Holy Spirit. She gazed upon the Most Holy Trinity, as one, in her contemplation: one God in three persons. This awe-inspiring vision bestowed upon her infinite joy, and she knew that this vision and joy would accompany her throughout eternity.

This abundance of divine grace is the promise that God holds for each one of us if we wholeheartedly love him with all our mind, heart, and strength. How can we attain it? Jesus has shown us the path: by striving to love him and our neighbor as he has loved us.

IV. An Earthly Mission Still Incomplete

(An Excerpt from Stronger Than Evil: The Devil: Recognizing Him, Overcoming Him, and Avoiding Him)

Behind every Marian sanctuary is a miraculous story linked to a prodigious image, an apparition, or the fulfilled vow of a people, a city, or an individual. They are stories of filial love, around which entire communities have been built.

There are Marian sanctuaries built on promontories over the sea, on hills overlooking seaside cities, and alongside ports. So many past sailors entrusted themselves to Our Lady at their local sanctuary for journeys that lasted years. Their families periodically visited the same sanctuary to entrust the lives of their loved ones to the capable arms of the heavenly Mother. In this sense, the ex-votos of sailors who emerged unscathed from shipwrecks or storms are fascinating and capable of telling, often in valuable artistic forms, how life, even the most banal, can be authentically imbued with faith and receive light and hope from a direct relationship with the transcendent.

These many stories and testimonies of faith, distributed over time and space, are born and develop in very different contexts. They never promote new doctrines but are a constant reminder of Jesus. Moreover, there is always an updating to the needs of the faithful in a particular time and place in which the apparitions or the miracle occurred that led to the construction of the sanctuary.

The center of these messages is always the Word of Jesus, and the worship that takes place in the sanctuaries is always centered on the Eucharistic Jesus. With immense pastoral effectiveness, these sanctuaries are a stimulus to conversion, prayer, and the reconciliation of peoples with Jesus and the Church.

The apparition in Guadalupe, which took place in the period following the discovery of the Americas, comes to mind. La Salette took place during a delicate moment in the history of Europe. Banneux, in the heart of Belgium, took place between the crises of the two world wars. Then there are the apparitions of Rue du Bac, Fatima with her extraordinary relevance, and Lourdes with her unfathomable testimony of love.

Our Lady reveals the way, provides succor, warns man against the foolishness of his ways, witnesses to the infinite divine mercy, and invites all to convert and entrust themselves totally to that mercy. Mary is the universal mediatrix of all graces. All graces pass through her, who protects each one of us.

One wonders what would have become of the faith of the French people today—so lacerated by Jacobin ideology—as well as the rest of Europe, without the three extraordinary apparitions that marked the first part of the nineteenth century: Paris in 1830, with Our Lady of the Miraculous Medal and the church of Rue du Bac, which is still the busiest in the French capital today; La Salette in 1846, with its prophetic message that anticipated that of Fatima; and Lourdes in 1858, with the confirmation of the dogma of the Immaculate Conception.

What would have become of the faith of the Portuguese without Fatima or of the faith of the Italians without the myriad Marian shrines scattered up and down the peninsula? These are places where the evangelical message resonates powerfully in the face of every heresy and perversity of the individual and of history. For this reason, St. John Paul II defined them as "permanent antennas of the good news."

Marian apparitions continue to this day, just as the construction of new Marian sanctuaries continues— in every corner of the world, even the most remote. This shows that Our Lady's earthly mission has never ended. It continues over the centuries, becoming more intense in certain periods, according to the needs of humanity. After all, Jesus' earthly mission is not over. He promised this himself, as we read in the Gospel: "I will not leave you orphans; I will come to you" (John 14:18).

Books by Fr. Amorth

From the Series: The Mission of Fr. Gabriele Amorth: Rome's Exorcist:

"My Rosary": The Beloved Prayer of an Exorcist. Icona Press, 2023. (Best Seller on Amazon)

The Life of Mary of Nazareth: Reflections of an Exorcist. Icona Press, 2024.

Did this book help you in some way? If so, we'd love to hear about it. Sincere reviews on **Amazon** and **Goodreads** help readers find the right book they are looking for.

About the Author

Father Gabriele Amorth (1925-2016), born in Modena, Italy, was a priest of the Society of St. Paul. He worked for thirty years as a journalist and editor for the Italian magazines *Familia Cristiana* and *Madre di Dio*. In 1986, he stepped down from his work in publishing after being appointed an exorcist of the Diocese of Rome. By his own account, he performed more than 60,000 exorcisms over the course of his thirty-year ministry. His work in the media discussing demonology and exorcism sparked renewed interest in exorcism. Today, he is recognized not only as the most well-known Catholic exorcist, but as one of the most prominent figures in the contemporary Italian Catholic Church.

About the Translator

Bret Thoman, OFS was born and raised in the suburbs of Atlanta, Georgia (USA). For the past ten years, he has lived in Loreto, Italy with his wife and three children. He has been a member of the Secular Franciscan Order (Third Order of St. Francis) since 2003. He has a master's degree in Italian from Middlebury College, a BA from the University of Georgia in foreign languages, and a certificate in Franciscan Studies. Bret is an FAA-licensed pilot and has logged over 3,500 hours of flight time.

Bret's main activity is organizing pilgrimages for St. Francis Pilgrimages, the company he founded in 2004. He leads individuals and groups through Italy, including to the friaries of Padre Pio in Southern Italy. He can be contacted at:
bret@stfrancispilgrimages.com

Bret has written and translated numerous books. All Bret's books are on Amazon at:
https://www.amazon.com/Bret-Thoman/e/B0753K2PTJ

www.ingramcontent.com/pod-product-compliance
Lightning Source LLC
Chambersburg PA
CBHW062008040426
42447CB00010B/1963